The Keyen of
FU TZE

The passing on of knowledge by the telling of tales is nearly as ancient as human knowledge itself. In many cultures the art of story-telling was an integral part of the transmission of history, philosophy and religion, and a source of great social entertainment.

Such stories are The Keyen of Fu Tze — the wise sayings of Confucious. Stories that present an image of the Way of Heaven, the Way that is without form and which cannot be described, and Fontenay leads the reader to feel that there is a path that slips through the logic and conditioning of the ordinary mind.

But this is no eulogy of the irrational. He declares "It is only when you have taken upon yourself the difficult task of teaching yourself that you can learn from Fu Tze". Drawing on Gurdjieffian ideas he suggests that the true way of man is neither in heaven nor on earth, but in himself, in all that is done when he is awake.

Illustrated by Sam Edelstein and set in fine Tiffany type, these are tales that give an insight into the mind of ancient China, a vital message about the state of mankind and a selection of seventy-seven stories that on any level make attractive reading.

THE KEYEN OF FUTZE

夫 子

Charles L. Fontenay

Coombe Springs Press

ISBN 0 900306 50 5
COOMBE SPRINGS PRESS
Sherborne House, Sherborne,
Gloucestershire.
GL54 3DZ
England

CHARLES L. FONTENAY

A journalist since the age of nineteen and at present re-write editor for The Tennessean in Nashville, Charles L. Fontenay was born in Sao Paulo, Brazil in 1917, of an English father and an American mother. He was brought up on a farm in Western Tennessee and at the age of twenty came across a copy of Ouspensky's "*Tertium Organum*". The book fascinated the young man, and its purchase was his first contact with the Gurdjieff work. This contact has continued for many years, and in 1974 after reading J. G. Bennett's "*A Spiritual Psychology*" Fontenay contacted Sherborne House, the home of the International Academy for Continuous Education, and it is from this contact that The Keyen of Fu Tze came to be written.

Fontenay is the author of several published novels and many short stories, and in 1969 completed ten years of study and research with the publication of a large philosophical work "Epistle to the Babylonians: An Essay on the Natural Inequality of Man". He has studied both German and Chinese, and in 1966-7 received a year's fellowship at Vanderbilt University, where he studied Chinese, philosophy, history and German; following it up with two additional years of Chinese language study. He began to practice the Korean style of karate in 1970, in 1975 received the black belt, and has just gained a 2nd degree black belt.

A married man with two children, Fontenay is at present working on his own translation of the *Tao Te Ching*. The format of this book stemmed from his interest in Chinese language and culture, in the martial arts, in Taoism and in his interest in the Chinese style of painting.

Foreword

Ke-yen" (pronounced "gé yen" in Mandarin Chinese—it would rhyme with "her yet") means "wise sayings". "Fu Tze" (夫子) means simply "The Sage". The name "Confucius" is an anglicization of "Kung Fu Tze," meaning "K'ung, the Sage".

In Chinese, "Fu Tze" means more than just an elderly man wise in the ways of the world. It is used in the sense of a sheng jen (聖人), a "master," one who is divinely inspired and intuitively wise. His wisdom does not apply to mundane matters such as business, politics, social morality and the like, but to matters — to use the vernacular — of "the soul".

This being the nature of the Sage, so is it also the nature of the "wisdom and immortality" — or, alternatively, "the Way of Heaven" — with which he is concerned. This state of being sought by the t'ao li is recognizable as that "transcendence" or "higher state of consciousness" that has been the goal of mystics in many cultures for many centuries.

The obliqueness of Fu Tze's answers to questions about this state of being is obviously deliberate — and necessary. Language was developed for the description and communication of that consensus interpretation of reality that fosters our adaptation to our contemporary culture; as Benjamin Lee Whorf pointed out, our language not only reënforces that "consensus reality" but actually has a great deal to do with shaping it. But "the Way of Heaven" is a different interpretation of reality, for which language was not formulated, and which thus cannot be described literally.

In order to comprehend what Fu Tze "really means," then, it is necessary to (a) remember that he is talking about this "different reality," and (b) note that his response is always to a specific question, exactly as it was put by the questioner.

CHARLES L. FONTENAY
Nashville, Tennessee

Contents

Illustrations

Illustrated by Sam Edelstein
Cover drawing by Charles L. Fontenay

夫子求乞米飯

1. FU TZE BEGS RICE

An Empty Rice Bowl

One day Yüan Chien*, who wanders constantly from the wastelands to the habitations of men and back again, paid a visit to an old friend, a beautiful and intelligent woman named Shen Chiao** who lived in Sinkiang Province. He found her very busy about the household, for she was possessed of a husband and children. It had been a long time since these two friends had talked of things strange and other-worldly, so Yüan Chien sat and sipped a cup of tea as they conversed, while Shen Chiao continued her chores about the house.

While they were talking, an old man came to the door of Shen Chiao's house, holding in his hand an empty rice bowl, begging. But Shen Chiao said sharply, "I have no time to stop and cook rice for you now, old man. Go away and come back when I am not so busy."

The old man turned silently and went away. Yüan Chien looked after him in astonishment, for he had seen on the old man's shoulder that fabled bird that is called 'chien' (鶼), which is divine but has only one wing and one eye, so that a pair of them must unite in order to fly.

"Do you not know that that old man is the Sage Fu Tze, for a single sight of whom many wise men would trade all of their riches?" asked Yüan Chien. "He is by far the wisest and greatest man you are ever likely to meet, and yet you treat him like a clumsy and ignorant country cousin, who must wait upon your convenience."

"Oh, yes, I know who he is," answered Shen Chiao carelessly, "I have known him for a long time. When I recognized that he was the Sage Fu Tze, I expected to learn great things from him. But if I am expected to be a servant to

* 遠見 : "Far sighted" or "Clairvoyant".

** 深交 : "Intimate Relationship".

cook rice for a man, I have a husband to serve. Besides, this Sage is not so wise as they say."

"Why do you say that?" asked Yüan Chien.

"Because I asked him a question, and he did not answer," she said. "All he did was to hold out his bowl and beg me to cook him rice."

"What question did you ask him?" queried Yüan Chien.

"I asked him how I might acquire wisdom and immortality," replied Shen Chiao.

Then Yüan Chien looked at her and spoke angrily.

"You are reputed to be a very intelligent person, and yet you have responded to a great Sage like a blind fool in the marketplace," he said. "Fu Tze answered your question.

"By asking you for rice to sustain his body, he told you that wisdom and immortality are not things of the mind and spirit alone, but require the participation of your body also. You responded by expecting an answer in words, which have no substance beyond your own thought.

"By asking you to cook rice for him when you were busy with household affairs, he told you that if you seek wisdom and immortality, you must value them above and before worldly matters. You responded by demonstrating that wisdom and immortality are of so little value to you that you will not interrupt your daily affairs for their sake.

"By asking you to serve his needs instead of discoursing with you about the mysteries known to him, he told you that the most direct way for you to acquire wisdom and immortality is to help him in his task. You responded by complaining that you are not a servant girl, and showing unwillingness to serve him occasionally in the same way that daily you serve an ordinary man.

"By coming to you as an old man, humble, with empty rice

bowl, he told you that before you can acquire wisdom and immortality, you must possess the natural grace to respect a Sage, however he may come to you. You responded by treating him as an ordinary beggar and making him wait upon your convenience.

"If Fu Tze had come to you as a learned teacher or a prince, in pomp and pride, speaking large words of obscure meaning, you would have prepared a feast of hung shao yü ch'ih* or pa pao ya** at whatever hour he wished, saying to your husband that the family must defer to the honoured guest. How strong is our presumption that Heaven will imitate the ways of man in its manifestations!

"The ways of Heaven are indeed strange that many wise men seek but a glimpse of Fu Tze in vain, and yet he has returned repeatedly to your door, though you have treated him with such unseemly condescension. Pray that Heaven may continue to overlook your folly yet one more time, else all that you have sought is lost for the inconvenience of preparing a bowl of rice."

*紅 燒 魚 翅 : Red-cooked shark's fin, a famous delicacy.
** 八 寶 鴨 : "Eight-jewel duck," duck cooked with certain spices.

A Door to Fit the Key

Upon learning that Fu Tze was in Sinkiang Province, Yüan Chien sought the Sage, and found him living in a hut near Hotien. As they drank tea together, Yüan Chien explained that he had wandered far and long in search of wisdom and immortality, and had heard the Way of Heaven expounded by many wise men, but was disturbed by one apparent contradiction in the different teachings with which he had come in contact.

"There are those who teach methods of resisting evil, to the point of dealing instant death in response to evil", said Yüan Chien. "There are also those who teach non-resistance to evil, to the point of accepting one's own death at the hands of evil. Yet the principles of both methods seem right to my ears.

"There are those who teach denial of the desires of the body, and there are those who teach the beauty of the body and its desires. Yet both teachings seem correct to my understanding.

"There are those who teach that one must isolate himself from other men in order to find wisdom and immortality, and there are those who teach that wisdom and immortality can be found only through one's relationships with others. Yet both ways seem reasonable to my heart as they are taught.

"Can you resolve these contradictions for me?"

"When a room has many doors, a man's search must be for that door that can be unlocked by the key in his possession", answered Fu Tze. "Because what matters to him is not the carving upon any door, but access to the room beyond it."

Upon receiving this answer, Yüan Chien determined to remain in Hotien to talk further with Fu Tze.

The School

Fu Tze lived simply and within himself, but Yüan Chien had not attained that eminence of wisdom. Yüan Chien, therefore, often frequented the teahouses and wineshops of Hotien, conversing with other men and women. When he met those who desired to attain wisdom and immortality, he would talk with them further and sometimes would invite them to accompany him in visiting the Sage.

One day while drinking wine with a man named I Chü,* Yüan Chien spoke to him of Fu Tze.

"I have heard of this old man and I have wished to ask questions of him", said I Chü, "for he is reputed to be a Sage. But he maintains no school or temple, nor does he seek disciples. How, then, can one learn from him?"

"Schools, temples and disciples are words that have meaning in the Way of the World", answered Yüan Chien. "In the Way of Heaven, you are your own school and your own temple, and you must be your own disciple.

"It is only when you have taken upon yourself the difficult task of teaching yourself that you can learn from Fu Tze."

* 夷 居: "Remains Squatting".

The Entrance Examination

As, for the purpose of his own further learning, Yüan Chien gathered a group of 't'ao li'* who spent much time in the presence of Fu Tze, they laboured to convert the ground around Fu Tze's hut into a garden of trees and flowers in which they might converse with each other and with Yüan Chien and Fu Tze.

There was among the 't'ao li' a woman named Ch'i P'eng** who had not come to Fu Tze's presence through acquaintance with Yüan Chien, but had learned of the Sage through her friendship with Shen Chiao. Ch'i P'eng also had sought wisdom and immortality for a long time and was anxious to spend much time in conversation with Fu Tze. Therefore, when Yüan Chien wished her to assist the other 't'ao li' in planting flowers in the garden, she was incensed.

"To become a gardener was not my reason for coming to this place", she said.

"Why, then, did you come?" asked Yüan Chien.

"To learn how to attain wisdom and immortality", answered Ch'i P'eng.

"Then you do not know already how to attain wisdom and immortality?" asked Yüan Chien.

"Of course I do not", said Ch'i P'eng. "If I knew already, there would be no need for me to come here."

"Then if you come here to learn something that you do not know", said Yüan Chien, "you are not qualified to say how what you wish to learn should be taught to you."

Recognizing the justice of his words, Ch'i P'eng said no more, but assisted the others in planting flowers in the garden.

* 桃 李: "peaches and plums" — therefore, the fruits of teaching: disciples, or younger colleagues.

** 奇 朋: "Rare Friend".

Wind and Rain

Ch'i P'eng, attaining great insight into the nature of wisdom and immortality and at the same time experiencing difficulties in daily life, was experienced enough in the Way of Heaven to recognize that the two circumstances were related. Yet, discerning no reason for such relationship, she questioned Fu Tze in the garden.

"If, as you say, the Way of Heaven is a reality, like the flowers and trees in this garden, why should our substantial steps along that Way be made only at the cost of emotional turmoil?" asked Ch'i P'eng.

The Sage led her to a series of clear pools connected by a stream that rippled through the garden. He pointed to the brightly coloured fish swimming in an upper pool.

"Why cannot those fish swim into the next pool, if they wish?" he asked.

"Because the water of the stream is dammed to form the pool", she answered. "The fish cannot go past the dam."

Fu Tze, taking brush and ink block, wrote upon the dam the characters 'feng yü': 封 魚 .* Then, beneath them, he wrote two further characters, 'feng yü': 風 雨 .**

"We shall return here tomorrow", said Fu Tze.

That night there came thunder and lightning and wind and heavy rain, and the trees in the garden bent to the force of the storm. The next morning, Fu Tze and Ch'i P'eng went again to the garden and he led her to the pool next below that one beside which they had walked the day before.

"Do you think that any of the fish that were in the first pool yesterday swim in this one today?" he asked.

* To seal in the fish.

**Wind and rain.

"I am sure of it", she said. "The rain was so heavy that it flooded the stream, and many fish must have been washed over the dam to the pool below."

"Great rains come only with storms", said Fu Tze.

How to Trap Wolves

To some of the 't'ao li' who complained that the circumstances of their ordinary lives made it difficult for them to follow the Way of Heaven, Fu Tze remarked that the circumstances of their ordinary lives would change if they themselves changed. But I Chü asked him how this was possible.

"The circumstances of our lives are imposed upon us by the conditions that surround us, which some say are the result of chance and others say follow the Will of Heaven", said I Chü. "How can my inner state affect conditions that are outside of me?"

"If your wolf-trap is baited with fodder", answered Fu Tze, "you will catch only sheep."

2. THE FISH GOES TO LOWER WATER

The Barrier

A man named Ti Lang* who had known Fu Tze earlier in Kwangtung Province came to Hotien to live among the 't'ao li'. Not having been before among people who sought wisdom and immortality together, he was surprised to find that the 't'ao li' often argued angrily among themselves.

"Why should this be, when all seek the same goal?" he asked the Sage.

"Once", said Fu Tze, "a man and a woman met in a bazaar in Samarkand. This man and this woman were so ideally suited to one another that, had they married, their love would have been a subject of legend for a thousand years and their children would have been princes and heroes.

"But they did not become friends, because the man spoke only Turkish and the woman spoke only Chinese, and each insisted that the other learn his own language if they were to converse."

* 弟 郎: "Younger Brother".

The Fearfulness of Kings

"The disagreements among the 't'ao li' are often very bitter", said Ti Lang. "If we faced such contentiousness among those with whom we deal in the Way of the World, we should go far away from them to avoid fighting them. Is not this an incorrect thing in the Way of Heaven?"

"Perhaps if you were older in spirit, it would be", replied Fu Tze with a smile. "But he who seeks the Way of Heaven must not shirk the company of dangerous and contentious men."

"How can this be", asked Ti Lang, "since the Way of Heaven is a path of peacefulness?"

"Once there was a king, Ti Lang, who was so fearful and insecure that he kept close watch upon the actions of the officials and courtiers who surrounded him", said the Sage. "Whenever one of these men showed by his actions or words that he disagreed with the king's opinions, he was executed or exiled. Therefore, none remained in that king's court who would challenge the king's will; but when an enemy brought armies against his kingdom, the king's advisors were of such inferior quality that he was dethroned and his kingdom conquered.

"There is within you, Ti Lang, as in all of us, a 'tzu kao'* which desires nothing but its own exaltation above others; and, because it sits upon a throne, we mistake that 'tzu kao' for ourselves. But if we are so fearful and insecure, like that king, that we surround ourselves only with those whose inferiority to us is obvious and shrink from associating with those who will fight us for the sake of truth, how shall we escape from the house of our pride?"

* 自 高 : Vanity, self-exaltation.

Gratitude

Shen Chiao was a very intelligent woman, but very obstinate. Finding fault with Fu Tze, she refused to consider him a Sage. Consequently, she did not become one of the 't'ao li', but sometimes visited Fu Tze's garden because of their long friendship, and sometimes Fu Tze visited her also at her home.

Yüan Chien once asked Fu Tze why it was that he continued to converse with Shen Chiao about the Way of Heaven, when she constantly disputed his words and criticized him.

"Shen Chiao once did me great injury", said Fu Tze.

"Why should that cause you to preserve your association with her", asked Yüan Chien in surprise, "unless you wish to avenge yourself by proving to her how wicked she was to injure a Sage?"

"If I had that motive, I would not be a Sage, and therefore my proof would be false", responded Fu Tze. "But by doing me that injury, Shen Chiao enabled me to increase my consciousness of true reality, therefore her action benefitted me and I owe her a debt of gratitude. Shen Chiao, however, remains aware of the nature of the injury itself, although she is so obstinate that she will not admit it, therefore Shen Chiao cannot increase her consciousness of true reality until she voluntarily makes amends to me for that injury.

"My debt of gratitude requires that I maintain association with Shen Chiao as long as she wishes to preserve it, so that she may have the opportunity to absolve herself of blame that still exists in her heart although it no longer exists in mine."

A Dirty Floor

Fu Tze was having tea with Shen Chiao while she, as usual, continued her household tasks.

"I do not understand why you retire to pursue the Way of Heaven when ordinary life is pleasant and interesting if one pursues it intelligently", she said.

"What are you doing now?" asked Fu Tze.

"As you can see, I am sweeping my floor", she answered. "Who desires to live in a house with a dirty floor?"

"Why is your floor more important to you than yourself?" asked Fu Tze.

Attention

How is it that you show Ch'i P'eng great favour, as one more advanced in the Way of Heaven than I?" asked Shen Chiao. "I knew you many years before Ch'i P'eng met you, and I have listened to you speak of these things much longer than she."

"Let us walk down by the garden", said Fu Tze.

The two of them walked at the bottom of the garden and looked at the plots of vegetables that had been planted and cared for by each of the 't'ao li'.

"Has not Hsin Hsüeh's plot grown well?" said Fu Tze. "Soon it will provide food for our table. I Chü's plot, here next to it, has not done nearly so well, and is badly choked with weeds."

"Obviously", said Shen Chiao, "I Chü did not water and weed and care for his vegetables as industriously as did Hsin Hsüeh."

"That is true", said Fu Tze. "I Chü was too preoccupied with other matters."

Fish

Among those who came sometimes to Fu Tze's garden was a woman named Su Yüan* who had known the Sage well when he was younger, but who had parted from him. So Su Yüan, being a friend of Ch'i P'eng and desirous of attaining wisdom and immortality, was persuaded by Ch'i P'eng to listen further to Fu Tze's words.

Su Yüan, however, doubted that Fu Tz'es knowledge in the Way of Heaven was of value to her, since their parting.

One day, Su Yüan was swimming with Fu Tze in a pool in the garden.

"I would be with you more often if it were convenient," said Su Yüan. "But the course I have chosen in the Way of Heaven involves me in the affairs of practical life, to which you are only incidental."

"Would you say that we who swim here are 'in' the water, or 'of' the water?" asked Fu Tze.

"Only in the water, of course", she said, laughing.

"And the fish in this pool?" asked Fu Tze.

"The difference is easily seen", answered Su Yüan. "They are of the water, because they cannot free themselves from it as we can."

Fu Tze left the pool.

"When you are no longer a fish, swim with me again", he said.

* 宿 緣
: "Predestined Mate"; it also can mean a destiny or affinity that is "sleeping" or inactive.

3. FU TZE LEAVES THE POOL

The Absentee

A young man named Hsin Hsüeh* who joined the company of the 't'ao li' in Fu Tze's garden was very quick of mind, and was deeply impressed with the Sage's wisdom. Yet after he had been among the 't'ao li' for some time, Hsin Hsüeh was disappointed to realize that his rational comprehension of Fu Tze's words had not caused him to see the world differently from before.

"Why is it", asked Hsin Hsüeh, "that I understand your admonitions for self-change, yet I seem unable to accomplish these things that you recommend?"

"No man can accomplish anything in his own absence", replied Fu Tze.

Since Fu Tze said no more than that, Hsin Hsüeh asked Yüan Chien if he could give a further explanation of the Sage's words.

"You do not understand what Fu Tze said because you think that you are here, now", answered Yüan Chien. "But that is an illusion. Almost always, you leave your body and the thoughts and feelings that belong to it care for themselves, while you wander elsewhere, either in the past or in the future.

"Until I speak of it to you, you do not know whether your neck and shoulders are relaxed or tense, you do not know whether your breathing is deep or shallow, you do not feel the sensation of your toes or see the colour of that which is before your eyes. If you do not remember yourself, but must have your attention called back to yourself by another person or by some illness or injury, how can you expect to do anything of your own volition?"

* 新 學 : "New Student".

Language

"We would be nearer to the Way of Heaven had we never learned a language with which to speak our thoughts to each other", said Fu Tze.

"How is that so, First Born, since teaching is done with words?" asked Ti Lang.

"That is why", replied the Sage. "It is more pleasing to our secret vanity to impart our knowledge of the Way of Heaven to others than to apply that knowledge to ourselves."

Appearances

"Many things you say violate teachings I have received elsewhere", said Hsin Hsüeh. "How can I know that you possess true knowledge?"

In reply, Fu Tze pointed to a nearby tree and walked away.

"Is that an answer?" Hsin Hsüeh exclaimed to Yüan Chien.

"Indeed", answered Yüan Chien. "Have you observed what kind of tree it was that Fu Tze indicated?"

"It is an apple tree", said Hsin Hsüeh.

"How do you know that?" asked Yüan Chien.

"Why, even if I did not know by its shape and its foliage, I can see ripe apples growing upon it", said Hsin Hsüeh.

"Very true; and you have been taught by your experience that these visible forms signify an apple tree", said Yüan Chien. "But could it not be, instead, an artificial tree with waxen apples, placed in this garden simply for decoration?"

"That is possible", admitted Hsin Hsüeh.

"Until you have tasted its fruit, you cannot know whether it is genuine", said Yüan Chien.

4. IS IT AN APPLE TREE OR NOT?

A Familiar Dream

"Lao Hsiung,*" said Yüan Chien to Fu Tze, "I have observed that for a time you had begun to enlighten Ch'i P'eng about certain matters in the Way of Heaven, but now you speak no more to her of these things. Why is this?"

"Because Ch'i P'eng cannot now hear what I have to say about these matters", answered the Sage.

"How do you determine that she is unable to hear?" asked Yüan Chien, for his relationship to Fu Tze was such that he was entitled to inquire about such things.

"Previously", said Fu Tze, "Ch'i P'eng had expressed to me certain convictions about these matters demonstrating that her view of them was one formed by her experience in the Way of the World. After a particular experience opened Ch'i P'eng's ears, I began to speak to her of these matters and she understood my words. But subsequently she repeated to me the same convictions as before, having modified her understanding to conform to them, therefore I spoke no more to her about these particular matters."

"However", said Yüan Chien, "what you told her of these matters during that period was only their beginning, and I know that what you had planned to elucidate further to her would clarify many of the questions upon which she bases her doubts. Therefore, if she understood what you have already told her, is not her subsequent lack of understanding simply a consequence of inadequate knowledge, and would it not be better to continue to speak to her of these matters so that more complete knowledge would improve her understanding?"

"Understanding must precede knowledge, Yüan Chien, not the opposite", said the Sage. "A seed sown on stony ground will not sprout."

* 老兄 : "Old Brother", a term of respect.

"But when the ground has been furrowed and the seed has sprouted, how can that field become infested with stones again?" asked Yüan Chien. "Explain to me why, First Born, if Ch'i P'eng acquired the capacity for understanding of these matters, she has not retained it."

"There are many Ch'i P'engs, just as there are at least two Yüan Chiens, one of whom remembers some of the things I have said to him and one of whom forgets", replied Fu Tze with a smile. "There was a Ch'i P'eng who would listen to her preconceptions in preference to considering the words of Fu Tze, and to that Ch'i P'eng I spoke little of such matters. Then a certain experience awakened a different Ch'i P'eng who, because of the understanding engendered by that experience, comprehended my words on such matters.

"Unfortunately, Yüan Chien, it is very difficult at first to stay awake in the Way of Heaven, because our most familiar emotions are associated with the dreams we dream in the Way of the World. Someone returned to Ch'i P'eng with a familiar dream, in which Fu Tze is only an eccentric old man, and the Ch'i P'eng to whom I spoke briefly about these matters has gone back to sleep lest that dream be disturbed.

"Therefore, Yüan Chien, I can only await her reawakening, because one who is asleep cannot hear clearly what I say."

5. THE CH'AO SINGS AT NIGHT

夜裡鼂唱歌兒

Songs in Darkness

The Sage Fu Tze has been likened to that legendary marine animal called 'ch'ao'*, which is said to sing by night and go into the sea by day. Thus, if you fear the dark, you can never hear his song.

* 鼂

Reputation

There was a man of Kwangtung Province who heard of Fu Tze's Wisdom and, being on a journey to Sinkiang Province, visited his garden and listened to some of his discourses. Afterward, being among the 't'ao li' and engaged in conversation with them, this man said he had known Fu Tze previously.

"Indeed, we were boys and young men together in Kwangtung Province," said the visitor, "though he did not go by that name there. He is but the son of a poor villager, with little education, and he and I were drunk together many times on rice whiskey and often wooed the village girls together. I admire his cleverness in going where he is not known and convincing people that he is a Sage, but I cannot consider it other then laughable that the uneducated son of a village labourer should pretend to knowledge of wisdom and immortality."

Because of what the stranger said about Fu Tze's past life, some of the 't'ao li' were disappointed and left him, but others remained with him.

The Black Prince and the Witch

When Yüan Chien returned to Hotien after an absence, he went first to the home of Wang Tzu* for a meal of 'hui kuo ju'** and rice. As they renewed acquaintance over that delicious Szuch'uan dish, Yüan Chien asked Wang Tzu of the Sage Fu Tze.

"I see Fu Tze only rarely now," said Wang Tzu.

"How is this?" exclaimed Yüan Chien. "When I saw you last in the Year of the Boar, you spoke of nothing but your great love and admiration for Fu Tze. Did you not tell me then that he had shown you beauty beyond any you ever knew?"

"That is so", admitted Wang Tzu. "And I spoke truth as I saw it then. But when I loved Fu Tze so greatly that I followed him without question, my admiration blinded my eyes. Only through suffering deeply for his sake did I realize that he is a dangerous man."

"I do not understand this", said Yüan Chien.

"Let me explain to you, Yüan Chien, that one who cannot give up life and go into the K'unlun Mountains as a monk in search of wisdom and immortality must exercise caution in dealing with a Sage", said Wang Tzu. "When my efforts to follow Fu Tze's sayings interfered with my business and endangered my domestic life, I saw at last that Fu Tze sought to seduce me into misguided ways."

"I can readily understand that Fu Tze would ask difficult things of you, which might violate the canons of common society, for such is the nature of the Way of Heaven that he teaches you", said Yüan Chien. "But I know that Fu Tze loved you also, and I cannot believe that he would lure you to your

* 忘 自 : "Forgot Himself".
** "Twice-cooked" meat.

detriment. Did he say nothing to you when you decided to leave the company of the 't'ao li'?"

"He but gave me this", said Wang Tzu, and handed Yüan Chien a strip of rice paper upon which were written the words 'wu ts'ui mien wang chih p'eng hsiang ti',* which can be read as, "In a room without a roof, purpose is lost (but) the sound of waves guides one to the proper path."

"What do you think is the meaning of that sentence?" asked Yüan Chien.

"I do not know", said Wang Tzu. "I feel sure that Fu Tze has criticized me for losing my former purpose and that he has spoken of a means of returning to what he considers my proper path. But I cannot interpret 'the sound of waves' unless it refers to the 'hai ch'ao',** the sound of Buddhist priests chanting; and I cannot believe that Fu Tze means to recommend that I follow the Buddhist Way."

"Surely", said Yüan Chien, "Fu Tze has spoken to you of remembering yourself?"

"Indeed", said Wang Tzu. "As you know, that Sage often says that we must pause frequently to remember who and what we are, or no teaching can help us."

"Often the words of a Sage cannot be taken literally", said Yüan Chien, "because the things that he seeks to show us are beyond the nature of common words to describe; but those who do not remember themselves can understand no other language. I believe that what Fu Tze desired to communicate to you does not lie in his written words, but in their sound."

Then Yüan Chien took a brush and wrote a sentence, 'wu

* 屋 摧 宀 亡 志 澎 響 迪

** 海 潮 : literally, "the ocean tide".

ts'ui mien wang chih p'eng hsiang ti',* having exactly the same sound as that which Fu Tze had written, but meaning, "The witch hypnotized the prince, causing friends to appear as enemies."

"That sentence is even more obscure than the other!" exclaimed Wang Tzu.

"But", said Yüan Chien, "it refers to the legend of a prince named Hsüan Yü** who was the heir to a great and beautiful kingdom. But one day the prince, while hunting in the forest, was ensnared by an evil Witch who wished to use him as a tool for her dark purpose.

"By her enchantment, the Witch convinced Hsüan Yü that his rich and beautiful kingdom was only a figment of his own disordered dreams and that her dark, drear underground world was the only true reality. She convinced him further that she, whose true form was as repulsive as a poisonous serpent, was a beautiful maiden of surpassing virtue who only wished his welfare and that all who had been his loyal friends and allies did but mean to seduce him to his harm.

"Therefore, when his friends came and would rescue him from the Witch's toils, Hsüan Yü himself drove them away with a sword.

"Woe to you, Wang Tze, for you have forgotten yourself! For the common world is like that Witch, having need of you for its own purposes, and it has woven an enchantment about you so that you have turned your back on the beautiful kingdom that is yours by right and have driven your friend, Fu Tze, from you with vulgar reproaches."

* 巫 催 眠 王 致 朋 像 敵

** 玄 玉 : "Black Jade".

A Beggar's Truth

There are those who say that you are a reincarnation of one of the Buddha's dearest disciples, while others say you are a wise man sent from a monastery hidden in the western mountains to teach", said I Chü. "How true are stories of this nature?"

"This is an idle question", answered Fu Tze. "If you would accept a truth from the Buddha but not the same truth from a ragged old beggar, that truth would be of no value to you."

Finding a Teacher

A man named Chiao T'ien* came to Fu Tze and said, "Honourable Sage, I have but one question to ask you. How can I find a teacher in the Way of Heaven?"

This question angered the 't'ao li', who felt that Chiao T'ien had thereby insulted Fu Tze, but the Sage quieted them.

"The owl hunts by night and the dog by day", he said. "Thus, it is no insult to the moon for the dog to consult it to determine when the sun will rise."

Turning to Chiao T'ien he said:

"Each day you move among many people, and one of them may be the teacher you seek. Among these many, you select only a few for conversation, or they select you, on the basis of your or their objectives for that day.

* 找 天 : "Seeks Heaven".

"If the man you seek as a teacher is not among those you select, it is because your objectives for that day are not such as to cause you to approach that man. If he is not among those who select you, it is because your objectives for that day are such that he is given no reason to desire to talk with you. And if you select him or he selects you, and yet you do not recognize him as the teacher you seek, that is because your objectives for that day are not those for which you seek that teacher.

"Therefore, Chiao T'ien, the answer to your question is that you will not find the teacher you seek by seeking for him among other men, but by seeking within yourself for your goal."

The Miser

Because it is required that we live like ordinary men in the world while we gain knowledge, I come to consult Fu Tze at the cost of great inconvenience", said I Chü. "But the things he tells me are things that I already know of my own thinking."

"Are you a wealthy man, I Chü?" asked Yüan Chien.

"You know that I am not", answered I Chü.

"Yet", said Yüan Chien, "the earth is full of gold."

Keeping Chickens

There was a man who came to Fu Tze's garden, desirous of joining the 't'ao li', but Fu Tze sent him away, saying that he must seek answers to his questions elsewhere. This action surprised the 't'ao li', and some of them asked Fu Tze why he had done this.

"The man has domestic problems, therefore he hoped to find emotional fulfilment among the 't'ao li', " answered Fu Tze. "His business is not prospering, therefore he wishes to try a less materialistic approach to existence."

"But many among us have domestic lives deserving of complaint, and none of us has been so successful in business as to become wealthy", said Ti Lang. "Do not all of us seek the Way of Heaven because we find the Way of the World unsatisfactory?"

"Yet you who are here have accepted your lot in the Way of the World before seeking the Way of Heaven", replied the Sage. "There may indeed be different reasons for keeping chickens, but unless one's pantry is full, he may always be suspected of being interested primarily in their eggs."

Questions

Yüan Chien has said that I do not gain more knowledge from your words because I do not ask the right questions", said I Chü. "But what kind of questions should I ask?"

"What is the colour of gold?" said Fu Tze.

The Butterfly

One day Hsin Hsüeh asked Fu Tze about the meaning of the words of that Sage, Chuang Chou,* when he dreamed of the butterfly.

"The meaning of Chuang Chou's words are contained in themselves, and I am not Chuang Chou, to add to them", demurred Fu Tze. "Also, Hsin Hsüeh, you yourself dream thus daily."

"Have you not told us, First Born, that different words are suitable to a different time and place?" responded Hsin Hsüeh. "Were Chuang Chou here now, perhaps he would say what he meant in other words."

"Were Chuang Chou here now, this would not be 'here, now'," said Fu Tze, "but I shall give you an answer.

"When you are in your store, Hsin Hsüeh, does not Hsin Hsüeh, who is here with me now as a seeker of wisdom and immortality, dream that he is a merchant? And when you cohabit with your wife, does not Hsin Hsüeh who is here now dream that he is a married man with children?

"Or is it that you are simply Hsin Hsüeh, the merchant and family man, who is now dreaming that he seeks wisdom and immortality in the company of a Sage?

"Which is the dream and which the reality, and who is the man dreaming? Does it not depend upon where you live most truly in yourself?"

* 莊周 : the Taoist Sage, better known as Chuang Tzu, who said that he dreamed he was a butterfly, but after he awoke, "I did not know whether it had formerly been Chou dreaming he was a butterfly, or it was a butterfly now dreaming that it was Chou. But between Chou and a butterfly there must be a difference. This is a case of what is called the transformation of things."

6. CHUANG CHOU SEES THE BUTTERFLY

Why Wu Wang Became Emperor

"What is the principle whereby we may hope to attain wisdom and immortality?" asked Ti Lang.

"Had Wu Wang* thought of himself as a peasant and the son of a peasant, he would have remained a servant of the Sung", answered Fu Tze. "Because he knew that his father was a king, and acted in accordance with that knowledge, he became Emperor of China."

* 武王 .Wu Wang's father, Wen Wang (文王), the legendary author of the I Ching, was ruler of the principality of Chou, but was imprisoned by Chou Hsin (紂辛), the corrupt last emperor of the Sung Dynasty. Wu Wang obtained his father's release and subsequently overthrew Chou Hsin to become the first emperor of the Chou Dynasty.

The Antagonism of Ts'ai Shen

"Lao Sou,* why do we sometimes imagine that you mislead us for your own selfish ends?" asked Hsin Hsüeh.

"You do not imagine that", answered Fu Tze. "You hear the voice within you of Ts'ai Shen,** the god of the Way of the World, and he speaks truth to those who follow him."

"How can both you and Ts'ai Shen speak truth, when Ts'ai Shen tells us that you are in no ways different from Tao Shen, + the god of robbers and thieves?" asked I Chü.

* 老叟 : "Venerable Sir".

** 財神 : "Mammon", the god of wealth and property; therefore, the inner representative of society's vested interests.

\+ 盜神

"Because Ts'ai Shen has erected a temple upon a hill, and only those confined within its walls are not evil in his eyes", said the Sage. "The followers of Tao Shen have naught in common with me, but, because both Tao Shen and I roam beyond the walls of Ts'ai Shen's temple, he does not differentiate between us."

"Although you show us Ts'ai Shen's faults, you do not urge us to fear and hate him", said Ti Lang. "Yet when Ts'ai Shen speaks within us, he causes us to fear and contend with you. Since you are antagonists, why this difference?"

"There were two men who dealt with animals", said Fu Tze. "Because the one man only wished to be friends with them, he attained his purposes by speaking with them and feeding them. Because the other wished to make them work for him, he whipped them so that they would fear to follow any will but his own."

"You advise us to continue to observe the legitimate directives of Ts'ai Shen in our daily life, lest we be alienated from our fellow men, warning us only not to worship Ts'ai Shen as the Shang Ti",* said Hsin Hsüeh. "Why, then, does that which is social and domestic within us, which you name as Ts'ai Shen, so violently oppose our learning the truth you speak?"

"When a man desires to water his fields, he takes a spade and diverts the river from its course", said Fu Tze. "When a man desires a guardian for his home, he takes a wolf cub and raises it from youth to be his servant.

"But a river that knows the truth about itself will refuse to be a canal, and a wolf that knows the truth about itself will refuse to be a dog."

* 上 帝 The supreme deity of heaven and earth; God.

Alertness Against Tigers

"You advise us to awaken to a more conscious state, yet one's purpose in being awake is only that one must tend one's garden or escape a tiger creeping from the forest", said Hsi Fang.* "The state of wakefulness is not in itself superior to the state of sleep, therefore, what is the purpose of being more conscious?"

"You have already stated it", said Fu Tze. "But, since you do not hear your own words, have you never heard anyone speak a reason for the desirability of becoming more awake than ordinary wakefulness?"

"That which I have heard, I do not consider adequate reason", said Hsi Fang. "There are those who call themselves teachers and those who call themselves priests and those who change their minds with drugs, all of them saying that their methods reveal a truer reality for their contemplation. But I do not consider contemplation in itself a worthy objective, else would it not be more desirable to contemplate an unreal but beautiful dream than to look upon a harsh reality?"

"In this you are correct, Hsi Fang", said the Sage. "For one cannot do anything but watch a dream unfold, while one may act upon reality. Therefore it is better in the Way of Heaven to help a blind man cross the street than to contemplate passively the greatest glory of the Infinite."

"That being so, Lao Hsiung, how will you answer my question?" asked Hsi Fang.

" 'Yang chih mi kao tsuan chih mi chien' ",**said Fu Tze. "There was a band of priests, Hsi Fang, charged with the

* 希 放 : "Strives for Liberation".

** 仰之彌高鑽之彌堅

: "By looking upward, you may comprehend height, but only by penetration can you comprehend substance."

preservation of a rich treasure in their monastery. Therefore, these priests did not seclude themselves behind the walls of the monastery, but moved constantly among the people of the town, teaching and doing good works. Thus it was not possible for robbers to congregate at the inns and plot to steal the monastery's treasure without the monks knowing of it.

"The priests and the treasure and the townspeople and the robbers are all within each of us. That is why I advise you to awaken and pay attention to the gossip of the townspeople."

Property

"Why is it", asked Hsin Hsüeh, "when one has accumulated knowledge and ability through many years, gaining him a measure of human recognition, this is considered inconsequential as an aspect of his true self? Has not this knowledge and ability been acquired as a consequence of the nature of the true self?"

"Yet it is still but an acquisition, and the acquisition must lack the wisdom of that which has acquired it", answered Fu Tze. "If you place your identity in something that is not yourself, you limit yourself to less than you are."

The Boastful Concubine

Because of her longer acquaintance with Fu Tze, Shen Chiao resented the 't'ao li's' attribution to him of superior knowledge.

"I value our friendship, but I have no need of your teaching", she said one day to Fu Tze. "For is it not said that one's only true teacher is within oneself?"

"Because you have said that to me, it is not true", answered Fu Tze. "But if I were to deny it to you, I would be lying."

These words puzzled Shen Chiao, therefore she asked Yüan Chien of their meaning.

"If a woman speaks of herself to a man as 'ch'ieh shen',* she but exhibits proper modesty, but if he addresses her as 'chien ch'ieh'** he does not compliment her", said Yüan Chien. "Therefore, what would have been correct for you to say to Fu Tze would have been incorrect for him to say to you.

"By saying to Fu Tze that you do not need his help in your search for wisdom and immortality, you have demonstrated a boastfulness that demonstrates that you are not ready for self-guidance; therefore you do need his knowledge very much. But if Fu Tze had answered that his knowledge is indispensable to your search, he would have exhibited a self-esteem that would have rendered his help of no value to you.

"It is true that your true teacher is within yourself, but you have just demonstrated that you are deaf to that teacher's admonitions."

* 妾身 : "Your concubine".
** 賤妾 : "My concubine".

Balance of Power

"Fu Tze taught that the 't'ao li' should free themselves from the inner compulsion to obey the customs of their culture, so that they could choose their own courses of action consciously.

"But are not culture and civilization those acquisitions of man distinguishing him most clearly from the beasts?" objected I Chü. "And are not men higher on the scale of existence than beasts? If we abandon that which distinguishes us from the beasts, then, do we not thereby become lesser creatures than we are, rather than greater?"

"Men and beasts are like two kingdoms, Jenlei and Tungwuchieh, that once were one", answered Fu Tze. "But Jenlei separated itself from Tungwuchieh because its customs were different and superior.

"In the kingdom of Jenlei, however, there were a few citizens who desired to separate yet further from these kingdoms because their customs were yet more different and superior. But they were so few that all efforts to separate and establish their own independent principality were suppressed by the authorities of Jenlei.

"At last they hit upon the idea of establishing their principality, which they called Omen, upon the border between Jenlei and Tungwuchieh. Thus, since their ways differed from the customs of both kingdoms, when the authorities of either kingdom attempted to force them into conformity with that kingdom's customs, the people of Omen could call upon the other kingdom for support. In this way, they maintained their independence from both."

Dragon Boat Warrior

"It appears to me that pride often is a good attribute, causing others to respect us and setting an honourable example for the young", said Ti Lang. "In what sense, then, do you say we should conquer our pride?"

"What you have said is true, and a man without pride seeking wisdom and immortality is a worm desiring the attributes of a tiger", said Fu Tze. "But a glass of wine may lift the spirits, yet a jug of the same drink demoralize the drinker.

"There was once a man named Kao Hsin* who contrived a mask to wear to the Wu Yeh Chieh.** This was a very cleverly carved mask, depicting its wearer as a warrior and a prince, and so impressive was its aspect that all at the festival treated Kao Hsin with deference.

"Now, Kao Hsin was one who was liked by his fellows, but he had never been treated with deference before. So when the Wu Yeh Chieh had ended, he did not take off the mask, but wore it when he returned to his daily duties. At first his friends laughed at this, but the mask was so impressive that gradually they began once more to treat Kao Hsin with deference.

"Kao Hsin, therefore, enjoying the deference he received, continued to wear the mask, and as time went on, he perfected himself in the behaviour of a warrior and a prince, appropriate to the mask he wore.

"Some of Kao Hsin's friends, who loved him best, urged him to take off the mask and wear it no more: 'for', said they, 'the natural growth and development of our friend Kao Hsin is a matter of importance to us, but that warrior and prince whose face is depicted by your mask is only an imaginary person.' But Kao Hsin would not remove the mask, lest others cease to pay him deference, and at last those friends who loved him best

* 高 心 : "Proud Heart".

** 五 月 節 : The Dragon Boat Festival.

left him in sorrow; for there was nothing of the Kao Hsin they loved in the warrior and prince depicted by the mask.

"So Kao Hsin lived, wearing his mask at all times, until there was no one who knew him who did not think he had been born a warrior and a prince. But then, as all men must, he died.

"And when those who came to prepare Kao Hsin's body for burial removed his mask, there was nothing behind it."

The Destiny of Apples

"It is true that all men are not equal in the capacity for understanding", said Hsin Hsüeh. "Yet all men are equally human, therefore it would seem that divine justice would provide the opportunity for all to attain wisdom and immortality."

Fu Tze pointed to an apple tree in the garden. The tree was laden with fruit, just beginning to ripen.

"What will happen to the apples on that tree?" he asked.

"The birds will eat some", answered Hsin Hsüeh. "Some will fall to the ground and be eaten by cattle and chickens. We ourselves will pick some, to eat now and to store for the winter."

"Also", said Fu Tze, "perhaps one or two of those apples will not be eaten up by the world, but will fall into a corner where they will lie in secret. Then, if the sun and the rain and the soil are right for this, they will sprout and no longer be apples, whose lives are but for a season, but trees that will live and produce fruit for many years.

"The different destiny of apples is the Will of Heaven."

The Destiny of Men

"Your words about the destiny of apples lead me to wonder if a man's success in achieving wisdom and immortality does not depend upon the caprice of heaven, like the fall of the apple", said Hsin Hsüeh. "If that is true, what can be gained by striving to achieve them?"

"An apple", replied Fu Tze, "can only hang on the tree until it falls, not by its own choice.

"Are you, Hsin Hsüeh, an apple?"

Justice

"I am still disturbed by the problem of justice that arises when, of two men, equally human, one has the capability and opportunity to attain wisdom and immortality but the other is denied both", said Hsin Hsüeh. "Whether through qualities acquired at birth or opportunities offered in the course of existence, does not Heaven thereby discriminate against the one man in favour of the other?"

"If all men were as the one man, possessing the capability and the opportunity, but only he achieved it, would you say that Heaven favoured him?" asked Fu Tze.

"No, of course not", said Hsin Hsüeh. "Obviously, in that case he would achieve it through his own effort, and the others could have done so through the same effort."

"And if all men were as the other man, possessing neither the capability nor the opportunity, would you say that Heaven discriminated against him because he, as all the others, failed to achieve it?" asked Fu Tze.

"Not at all", replied Hsin Hsüeh. "For the inability to achieve it would then be of the nature of men, even as we do not now attribute to the lower animals the possibility of achieving wisdom and immortality."

"Yet we do not think of Heaven as unjust in denying it to the animals", said the Sage. "It is the justice of man that measures one man against another. The justice of Heaven measures a man only against himself."

A Letter to T'ienmen

Hsi Fang spoke in defence of Shen Chiao to Fu Tze. "For", said Hsi Fang, "she is interested in the Way of Heaven, saying only that her domestic duties are her first responsibility. And, though we are expected to consider the Way of Heaven first, you insist that the 't'ao li' also fulfil their responsibilities in wordly affairs. Is the difference so great that you are justified in criticizing her?"

The Sage did not reply to Hsi Fang at that time, but a few days later met him in the street in Hotien. Hsi Fang carried a letter in his hand, and Fu Tze inquired about it.

"It is a letter to my cousin in T'ienmen", said Hsi Fang. "I am on my way to mail it."

"Since I am planning to go to T'ienmen, why do you not let me take it and deliver it, saving you the cost of postage?" suggested Fu Tze. Surprised that Fu Tze should coincidentally be going to T'ienmen at this time, Hsi Fang thanked him and gave him the letter.

But some days later Hsi Fang came to the hut of Fu Tze, and found the Sage at home, while Hsi Fang's letter to his cousin still lay in view on a table. Hsi Fang was incensed.

"How is this, Lao Sou?" he asked. "Did you not tell me that you were going to T'ienmen, and would deliver this letter for me there?"

"Indeed so", answered Fu Tze. "I am planning to go to T'ienmen as soon as I can devise a way to do so without leaving Hotien."

"But that is impossible!" exclaimed Hsi Fang.

"Yet", said Fu Tze, "in the Way of Heaven, Shen Chiao is so attached to Hotien that she will not go to T'ienmen unless she can do so without leaving it; while the 't'ao li', though they live fully in Hotien while there, leave it freely to go to T'ienmen. That is the difference of which you spoke."

The City Within

"What is the most difficult illusion we must overcome in seeking wisdom and immortality, while yet remaining involved in wordly affairs?" Hsin Hsüeh asked Fu Tze.

"It is understanding that we must travel to T'ienchin,* not from Chiuchinshan** but from Humen", + replied the Sage.

"The only interpretation I can place upon Fu Tze's answer to my question is that we are not as far from wisdom and immortality as we think", said Hsin Hsüeh to Yüan Chien.

"You have reversed the Sage's words", said Yüan Chien. "It

* 天津 : Tientsin, a port in Hopeh Province.
** 舊金山 : San Francisco.
+ 虎門 : Humun, a port in Kwangtung Province.

is Chiuchinshan that is a foreign city, while Humen is in China, as is T'ienchin.

"We all know that the Way of Heaven is within us. But we think that the Way of the World, from which we must depart to achieve the Way of Heaven, exists outside of us; yet it, too, is within us."

A Tale of Two Cities

"I have noticed", said Hsin Hsüeh, "that you urge Ti Lang to practice correct conduct, to work faithfully at his profession and consider his responsibilities as a family man; but to Su Yüan you recommend that she act in ways that would be disapproved by the community if known. Is not the Way of Heaven the same for all, and does not this advice in fact represent different goals?"

"Neither constitutes a goal", answered Fu Tze. "One may go southeast from Peiching and another northwest from Ch'ingtao and both be going to T'ienchin. But neither can reach T'ienchin if they do not leave the streets of Peiching and Ch'ingtao."

Hsin Hsüeh thanked the Sage for his words, but later said to Yüan Chien, "the manner in which Fu Tze's answer applies to the question I asked him is not entirely clear to me."

"Know then, Hsin Hsüeh", said Yüan Chien, "that the pathways of your mind and heart have been trodden and retrodden in the experiences of your life until they are as familiar to you as the streets of your home city. You walk them without the necessity of thinking when you turn and where you cross.

"Fu Tze's meaning was that the history of Ti Lang's city began with discord and fighting in the streets, and the signs at every corner cry rebellion against the authorities; but in Su Yüan's city, each revolt has been suppressed and the soldiers of the Manchu tyrants patrol every street, so that she walks carefully each time she goes forth from her walled courtyard, lest she be charged with the transgression of some ordinance.

"But one cannot reach T'ienchin, the Port of Heaven, except along roads that go forth beyond the streets of his own city. Therefore, Fu Tze has recommended to Ti Lang that he make peace with the authorities and treat them with correctness, so that civil strife will not hinder his passage along the road to T'ienchin. But he has advised Su Yüan that the authorities of her city are so oppressive that she must evade them by way of back streets if she is to escape through the gates and find the road to T'ienchin."

Intimate Rain

The Sage Fu Tze is sometimes called 'mi yü',* because he is like the rain falling quietly upon the earth. Those flowers kept inside, where the rain cannot reach them, do not grow.

* 密雨 : "Secret" or "intimate" rain; thus, a misty rain.

The Insistent Host

"The customs and morality of a culture are not all restrictive and irrational, but often contain desirable patterns of conduct", said Ti Lang. "In advising us to free ourselves from them, do you not contemplate that we would sacrifice many good things in order to divest ourselves of a few bad things?"

"To free yourselves from the habitual compulsion to follow them is simply to put yourselves in a position where choice is possible", answered Fu Tze. "Would you wish to eat the rarest delicacy at a feast, were it forced upon you by your host rather than served to you as a result of your own taste for it?"

Relations with Heaven

"Most teachers of exceptionally high spiritual reputation emphasize the necessity of submitting humbly to the Will of Heaven and giving up personal identity", said Hsi Fang. "Why do you not also do this?"

"There is no advantage to Heaven in your humility", replied Fu Tze, "for the Will of Heaven will be done in any case, and you will submit to it. Therefore, the only question for you to consider is advantage to yourself.

"When you consider advantage to yourself, you must remember that the Way of Heaven is not as the Way of the World, but always leads in opposite directions at the same time.

"It is the Will of Heaven that men differ for the carrying out of its purposes, else men would not differ. Therefore, since the wisest of men cannot know the purpose of Heaven, may it not be the Will of Heaven that one man rebels against that to which another man submits?

"To submit voluntarily to the Will of Heaven insofar as you understand its purpose correctly is advantageous to you, for one travels faster with the storm-wind than against it.

"But to rebel against the Will of Heaven when its purpose seems to you incorrect is justified, for a boat would not be given a rudder were it meant simply to drift with the wind."

Night Must Fall

"Why do you always urge us so insistently?" I Chü, in a cross temper, asked Fu Tze. "We have many practical responsibilities and, after all, we have all the rest of our lives in which to achieve wisdom and immortality."

"Very well", said Fu Tze. "For today, I will ask of you a practical task. Please go and plant that garden."

"I shall begin that task willingly", answered I Chü. "But I cannot complete it today. It is too late, and will soon be night."

"But if you had worked at it earlier, you could have finished it before darkness falls", said the Sage.

A Lesson in Gymnastics

"The things that you say are intelligible to me, and yet I cannot see that my comprehension of your words results in any change in my state of being", said I Chü. "What is the reason for this?"

"Can you become a gymnast by listening to lectures on the physical laws of balance?" asked Fu Tze.

~

Inertia

"By making the effort to remember what and where I am, I have been able to achieve the state of awareness that is called 'detachment' ", said Hsin Hsüeh. "But I can maintain that state of awareness only briefly. It is as though great pressure were being exerted on me by all of the reality around me to return to my usual state of dreamlike absorption in illusion."

"No matter how far a stone is pushed uphill", responded Fu Tze, "it will always roll back to the bottom until it is pushed over the crest."

The Origin of Centaurs

"I do not understand exactly what 'detachment' is, or how we can practice it and still continue worldly activity while seeking wisdom and immortality", said Ti Lang.

"There was once a horseman who so loved to ride that he became a horse", answered Fu Tze, "and thus Centaurs originated."

"Now, how can I understand 'detachment' from that saying", Ti Lang said to Yüan Chien, "since Centaurs do not exist?"

"Centaurs do not exist only in places where men do not ride horseback", said Yüan Chien. "I have heard the Sage answer that question differently: 'Once there was a merchant who so loved buying and selling that he became his store. And his wife so loved beauty and convenience of their home that she became that house. Often in the world, one does not find a man and a woman, but a store married to a house.'

"Now, Ti Lang, do you understand Fu Tze's saying?"

Going into Battle

"Can you tell me in a few words the meaning of 'wisdom and immortality' and how one may attain them most quickly?" Ti Lang asked.

"Once there was a horseman who so loved to ride that he became a horse", answered Fu Tze, "and thus Centaurs originated."

"But that is the same answer you gave me when I asked the meaning of 'detachment'! Ti Lang exclaimed. "Is it then necessary only to achieve detachment to acquire wisdom and immortality?"

"No, for the method is not identical with the goal of the method", said Fu Tze. "But when one tosses a coin to a beggar, it may fall heads-up one time, tails-up another time."

"That answer is completely incomprehensible to me", Ti Lang said to Yüan Chien.

"It should not be", replied Yüan Chien. "If a man labours in the field, wearing old clothes, and yet remains aware that he is a scholar of the Classics and a friend of princes, that is 'detachment'. But if, going into battle, he becomes completely a soldier lest he be killed, that is 'wisdom and immortality'."

The Hunting Tiger

"How can a physical exercise like the T'ai Chi Ch'uan* be of any value in the search for wisdom and immortality?" asked Hsin Hsüeh.

"In the Way of the World", answered Fu Tze, "wisdom and immortality are but wishes and the T'ai Chi Ch'uan is but the dream of being a stork, a snake and a tiger. But the movement of the tiger when he hunts is more than a wish or a dream.

"Observe, then, Su Yüan when she walks among men, knowing that she is seen. She walks carefully and with dignity, as befits the wife of a government official. But what has the wife of a government official to do with wisdom and immortality?

"The purpose of movement is to carry the body to a goal."

* 太極拳
: Chinese method of bodily training.

相好

Of Books and Sages

In their past association, there had existed 'hsiang hao'* between Fu Tze and Su Yüan, and the Sage, because of his continuing feeling toward this woman, wished the relationship to be resumed; Su Yüan, however, was reluctant. This condition of their hearts was apparent to the 't'ao li', who differed in their attitudes with respect to it.

"The Sages of whom I have read were above the desires of the world as the white crane in the clouds", said Ch'i P'eng to Fu Tze. "How, then, can you be a true Sage and desire Su Yüan?"

Fu Tze handed her a book and commanded, "Read to me of the strange destiny of the woman, Jade Incense."

Ch'i P'eng looked at the book and said, "I cannot, for this

* 相好
: A lasting sexual relationship without formal marriage.

夫子請奇朋給朗誦一本書

7. FU TZE ASKS CH'I P'ENG TO READ A BOOK ALOUD

book is not 'Yü Hsiang Ch'i Yüan',* but the 'Hsiao San Kuo Chi'h."**

"Ah", said Fu Tze. "Then have you decided what you wish for your breakfast today?"

"I would like 'chi tan ch'ao fan'," + said Ch'i P'eng.

"Very well", said Fu Tze, and pointed to the chicken-yard. "Put saddle and bridle on that old hen, ride her to the stables and gather the eggs the horse has laid."

Ch'i P'eng, being wise in the methods of the Sage, repeated what he had said to Yüan Chien, saying: "I know that Fu Tze has answered the question I asked him, but I do not understand his reply."

"He told you that when you read of Sages, what you read is that which is in the book, and no more", replied Yüan Chien. "He also told you that all Sages are not of the same nature, and if you desire something from a Sage, you should not expect to gain from one what only another can give you."

* 玉 香 奇 緣
: "The Strange Destiny of Jade Incense."

** 小 三 國 志
: "The Small Chronicle of the Three Kingdoms."

± 鷄蛋炒飯
: Eggs scrambled with rice.

夫子在太陽光裏站立

8. FU TZE
STANDS IN
THE SUNLIGHT

The Shadow

Once when Fu Tze had wooed Su Yüan with persuasive words as a young man woos a maid, Su Yüan, refusing the Sage's wishes, said to him: "I fear that you attach too much importance to the body. When I would meditate upon the processes of the Way of Heaven, you tell me to sit naked and be conscious of my breath. When I say that my love for you is of a higher nature than that between a woman and a man, you urge me to share 'yün yü* with you."

Fu Tze arose from the table at which they shared tea, and stepped into the sunlight, so that his shadow lay upon the ground before him.

"How important is my shadow?" he asked.

"It is not important at all", she answered, smiling.

"You are wrong", he said. "If there were no shadow here, it would mean either that I were not here or that the sun which gives me life did not shine in the sky.

"But, by looking at my shadow, can you tell the colour of my eyes?"

* 雲 雨 : "Clouds and rain," a euphemism for sexual intercourse. From the legend of a prince who climbed Mount Wu in eastern Szechwan and fell asleep. He was visited by the Lady of the Mountain, who commands the clouds in the morning and the rain at night, and she shared his couch with him.

The Rosebush

Fu Tze, in admiration of Su Yüan's beauty, plucked a rose in the garden for her hair. As he did so, he murmured a phrase of apology and gratitude to the rosebush.

"Why do you do that?" asked Su Yüan. "The rosebush cannot hear you."

"As to that, you do not know, nor do I", he answered. "But I thank the rosebush lest I be denied immortality for forgetting that it does not belong to me, but to itself."

Improper Conduct

Su Yüan could not determine for herself whether Fu Tze, whom she had known in different days, was truly a Sage or merely an ordinary man. But she reasoned that, if he were an ordinary man, there were no profit to her in resuming 'hsiang hao' with him; whereas, by the teachings that she had acquired in the Way of the World, 'hsiang hao' would constitute improper conduct for a Sage. Therefore she told him that she found no ground for acceding to his wish.

Fu Tze was overcome by sadness at her refusal, and retired to the forest to meditate. His action was disturbing to some of the 't'ao li'.

"How is it that one wise in the Way of Heaven should be affected in this manner by a woman's refusal?" asked I Chü. "This is in no way different from the reaction of any ordinary man in the same situation."

"Why should that surprise any of us?" responded Yüan Chien. "In relation to us, Fu Tze is a Sage, but he cannot look upon himself as a Sage, but only as a man; for a Sage to Fu Tze would be someone who could assist him as he assists us, possessing superior knowledge in the Way of Heaven.

"Perhaps, I Chü, you feel that it would be more to your profit to learn from one whom Fu Tze would consider a Sage. But that is not true. One whom Fu Tze would consider a Sage would be so far beyond you that you could not understand him at all."

Volition

When Su Yüan refused to reëstablish 'hsiang hao' with Fu Tze, she left the company of the 't'ao li;' for, turning her heart against the Sage where formerly it had turned toward him, she said, "Fu Tze arrogantly assumes to himself the responsibility for showing me the way to attainment of wisdom and immortality, but I do not need his assistance in this."

Ti Lang, who loved Fu Tze more personally than the other 't'ao li' because of their long friendship, was angered, and expressed his anger to the Sage.

"I know that you possess knowledge beyond ordinary knowledge", said Ti Lang. "Since she has acted unreasonably, and yet your heart has need of her presence, are you not justified in using that knowledge to influence her to return and look upon you with favour, believing that she does so of her own volition?"

"Should I do that, I would thereby prove Su Yüan to be right in her accusation against me", replied Fu Tze. "And, were she right, she would be justified in turning her heart against me and leaving the company of the 't'ao li'."

"But is she not right in fact, if wrong in accusation?" asked Ti Lang. "For is it not your responsibility to teach her, since she is capable of learning?"

"Only if she accepts my gifts voluntarily", said the Sage, "for then I also gain in wisdom and immortality, through giving of it. But I gain nothing if I sow seed in soil where it will not grow and return fruit to me."

"That is a hard saying!" exclaimed Ti Lang. "I know that you love Su Yüan. Loving her, how can you adhere to such requirements when the matter of her immortality is involved?"

"Love cannot confer immortality upon another, but only upon oneself", answered Fu Tze. "In the Way of Heaven, one may not take upon oneself the task of another's immortality, for it is task enough to achieve one's own."

How to Change the Past

"It is said that one who is a great Sage has conquered time, and is able to change the past", said I Chü to Fu Tze. "I wish that I had that power."

"What in the past would you change?" asked Fu Tze.

"For many years I sought wisdom and immortality without success, before I was led to your presence", answered I Chü. "Could I change the past, I would alter my life so that I might find you earlier and thus be more advanced in my understanding of the Way of Heaven before my inevitable death."

In answer, Fu Tze took a stick and wrote in the dust two characters resembling I Chü's name in their sound, but with the meaning "the fierce dog seizes".*

"There is a story told about a dog who had a cruel master", said Fu Tze. "The dog complained to Heaven that it was his fate to belong to this wicked man, but his supplications brought no change in his condition. At last, although he knew that he thus guaranteed his own death as a dangerous animal, he seized his master by the throat and killed him. As that man was dying, he exclaimed, 'How foolish I have been to harbour this fierce dog in my house! Never again will I own a dog!' And, of course, he never did."

The 't'ao li' laughed at Fu Tze's joke, but I Chü was dissatisfied. After they had left the Sage's presence, he complained to Yüan Chien, "Why is it that when I ask Fu Tze for the knowledge to change the past, he answers me with a joke? Is it that I am not worthy of that knowledge?"

"You are not worthy of it if you do not understand what he said", answered Yüan Chien. "For when Fu Tze wrote those characters in the dust, he contrasted their meaning with the meaning of your own name, which is 'to remain squatting', signifying a useless life.

* 猗 據

9. THE FIERCE DOG ATTACKS ITS MASTER

"Surely you have been present when Fu Tze taught that it is only in moments of great emotion or passion that one possesses the extraordinary energy to defy successfully the laws that bind us to the Way of the World. The moment of death is such a moment, and the irreversibility of time is such a law.

"When the dog only complained to Heaven of the past, without doing anything more, he accomplished nothing. The only time anyone can change anything is at the present moment. But when the dog, in a passion that defied his own death, seized and killed his master, he caused the master to wish in the moment of death the same thing that the dog wished: that he had never owned the dog.

"Those who are bound by the Way of the World and time see only a joke in the story, because of course the man never again owned a dog, after his death. But those who are aware of the circular nature of all existence will see beyond the joke.

"Understanding, I Chü, that you can act only in the present, have you ever, through your own passionate commitment, caused Fu Tze to desire with equal passion that you should have met an earlier time in both your lives?"

The Magical Elixir

"Lao Sou, I have learned that from you which you did not teach", said I Chü. "I have learned that the practices and principles you have revealed to us can give power in the Way of the World. What is to prevent our using this knowledge for worldly purposes instead of for the achivement of wisdom and immortality?"

"Let us imagine that a man has a single, lovely daughter, who is ill of a rare disease that is inevitably fatal", said Fu Tze. "Then a magician gives the man a small bottle filled with golden liquid. The magician tells the man that this is all of that liquid that exists in the world, and it is the only thing that can cure his daughter; but if the man will drink it himself, he can become emperor of the world.

"Will the man use the liquid to cure his daughter, or to become emperor of the world?"

"There is no doubt in my mind that he will use it to cure his daughter", replied I Chü.

"You have answered your own question, as far as I Chü is concerned", said Fu Tze. "But only that: because you do not know the man whom the magician approached."

Generosity

Hsin Hsüeh and I Chü were arguing about the story told that the Greek Diogenes was approached by Alexander the Great, who asked that Sage what he could do for him; whereupon Diogenes suggested that the conqueror might well stand aside, since he was shading Diogenes from the sun. Hsin Hsüeh contended that Diogenes thereby sought to demonstrate to Alexander that even the master of the world was less important than the sunshine, while I Chü argued that Diogenes was simply exhibiting pettishness and arrogance.

At last they asked Yüan Chien for his opinion.

"Perhaps you will understand it better if I relate to you a similar occurrence involving your own friend, Fu Tze", answered Yüan Chien.

"One time a wealthy and powerful man visited Fu Tze, and, admiring the Sage's wisdom, wished to do something for him. He suggested to Fu Tze that he might purchase for him a larger, more comfortable house and a more extensive garden, or perhaps use his influence with government officials to gain recognition for him, so that his wisdom might be known more widely.

"Fu Tze thanked the man, but replied, 'Since none of the 't'ao li' are here tonight and I have much writing to do, if you really wish to help me, you may prepare the evening meal'.

"In the Way of the World, the giver is made to feel important by the nature of his gift, but in the Way of Heaven, generosity is determined by the willingness to give what the recipient most desires."

Ways and Means

"We are told that we should not be guided by the desires of the body, and yet many actions you advise are designed for the satisfaction of the body's desires", said I Chü. "We are told that we should not be ruled by our emotions, and yet many decisions you advise are those dictated by the heart. We are told that we cannot rely on rationality and reason, yet you advise us to think independently and question for ourselves everything that you tell us."

"A man without legs must ride", replied Fu Te.

"What is the meaning of this saying?" I Chü asked Yüan Chien.

"If you had no legs, you could not get across the city except by riding in a carriage", said Yüan Chien. "Therefore, you would insist that the carriage receive grease and paint and all that it needed to keep it running smoothly and comfortably, but you would not go hungry in order that the carriage might have a new coat of paint.

"You would insist that the horse be fed and groomed so that he would remain strong and healthy in order to draw the carriage, but you would not allow him to be hitched to the carriage without reins, to return to the barn or meadow at his will when you were riding to some destination of your own.

"You would require that the driver know his way about the city, and pay him well so that he could support himself and his family, but when you wished to go across the city you would not permit him to drive you elsewhere or stop at the inn at his own pleasure.

"You do not yet possess legs to walk the Way of Heaven, therefore you must consider the needs of those vehicles that bear you along that Way, as well as your own desire to attain your destination."

Building

"I have known people who are conscientious and sincere in doing good to their fellow men", said Ti Lang. "I have known others who were honestly devout in their religious feelings. I have known yet others who sought assiduously to free themselves from the Way of the World by ecstatic meditation, by employing drugs to alter the way in which they discern reality, by mortification of the flesh, and by other means. Yet it is obvious that none of these has achieved wisdom and immortality. Why is this?"

"A carpenter may work very hard at sawing boards and nailing them together", answered Fu Tze. "Yet, if he lacks the plan of a house, he will never build a house by means of all his labour."

"On the other hand", said Hsin Hsüeh, "I have known some people whose understanding of the nature of wisdom and immortality was very profound. Yet, neither had they achieved wisdom and immortality."

"An architect may draw workable plans for the most magnificent mansion the world has ever seen", replied the Sage. "Yet, if those plans remain but a diagram on paper or an image in his mind, that mansion will not exist. Until the hammer has been put to the nail, the architect will still be without a roof over his head."

Identification

"Your problem", said Fu Tze to the 't'ao li', is that each of you is as inseparable from himself as the 'chü ch'iung',* which consort with the 't'iao shu'** and carry it away at the first sign of danger. That 't'iao shu' is your false pride."

"How can one not be inseparable from himself?" asked Hsin Hsüeh. "Does this have to do with what is called 'detachment'?"

"It has to do with whatever you choose to discuss", replied the Sage. "Put your hands to your head, Hsin Hsüeh, and feel your skull."

Hsin Hsüeh did as he was bidden.

"To your hands, there is nothing to distinguish what they feel from the head of a stranger", said Fu Tze. "It is only the net of your thoughts that entraps you within that skull, for your hands are wiser than your mind. You are involved in the affairs of your mind and heart and body as one who, watching a well-played drama upon the stage, weeps at the sorrows of the heroine.

"But if you would find the Way of Heaven, Hsin Hsüeh, you must treat yourself in the same manner as you treat others."

* 駏蛩 : Two legendary animals of the northern plains, one resembling a horse, the other a mule, whose names are used to indicate inseparable attachment.

** 跳鼠 : The jerboa, or jumping rat.

10. THE CHÜ CH'IUNG IN THE NORTHERN DESERT

The Three Kingdoms

One of the 't'ao li' was known as Ts'ung Ming,* because he was so intelligent that he grasped the principles that Fu Tze enunciated more quickly than any of the others. But Ts'ung Ming fell in love with a young woman of Hotien, who at first encouraged him but later turned from him to another. Ts'ung Ming was very unhappy about this, and for a time he abandoned the discourses in the Sage's garden to mope in the winehouses of the city.

When Ts'ung Ming returned to the garden, he asked Fu Tze, "Why is it, Lao Sung, that I am so intelligent that my brothers and sisters here admire my brilliance, yet my intelligence does not serve me well in an ordinary relationship with a woman, in which even stupid men excel?"

"In the days of the Three Kingdoms", answered Fu Tze, "there was a man who lived in the Kingdom of Wei, which was dominant among them. Because he lived in the most powerful of the kingdoms, the conditions of his existence were favourable and he prospered. But one time when he was on a journey to the Kingdom of Shu, hostilities broke out between these two kingdoms and the man was seized as a stranger and an enemy, and was put to death.

"Yet had this man lived during a time when the land was united under a strong emperor, he could have travelled anywhere in the territory of the Three Kingdoms without risk.

"You, Ts'ung Ming, think that you are man undivided, like the land united under an emperor. But you, like most men, are divided into three kingdoms, which are independent of one another and often contend one with the other. They are called T'ou, Hsin and Shih.**

* 聰 明
: "Intelligent".

** Head, Heart and Body.

"You live most of your time in the Kingdom of T'ou within yourself, and it is because you are so familiar with it that your intelligence is recognized as superior. But in order to conduct a relationship with a woman, it is necessary that you travel to the Kingdom of Hsin, where you are a stranger and likely to suffer severely in case of contention between the two."

Point of View

Sometimes when I act, I think I am following the Way of Heaven, but I then realize I have followed the Way of the World in that action; at other times, I think I only follow the Way of the World, but find that I have followed the Way of Heaven", said I Chü. "How does this happen?"

Fu Tze took a stick and in the dust drew a picture of a flight of stairs:

"Were you to set foot upon these stairs from this end that is nearest to us, would you then climb up or down?" he asked.

"That is quite clear", answered I Chü. "I would walk up the stairs, for I look at them from a position to the right and above them."

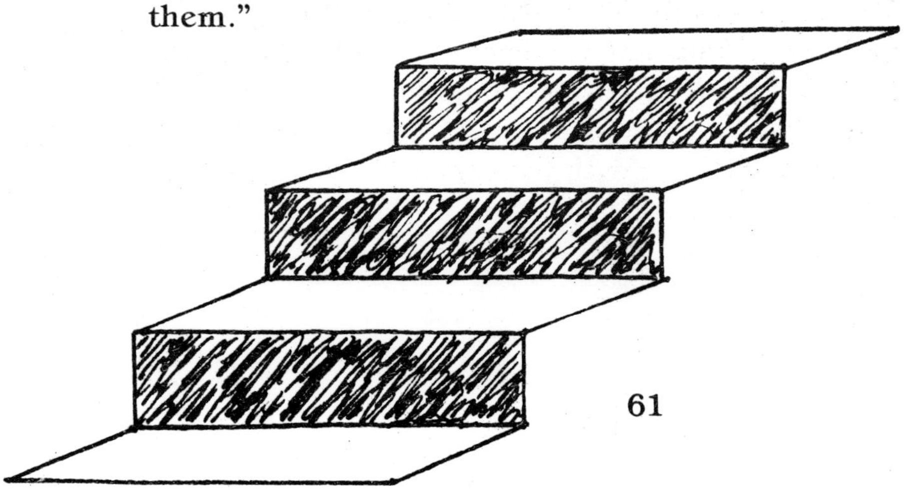

"Not so", disagreed Shen Chiao, who was present. "It is plain to see that we look at the stairs from beneath, so that in order to enter them from this end it would be necessary to step first upon the top step."

"You two are equally right and equally wrong", said Fu Tze, "because you do not see real stairs but only a picture of stairs."

Forgiveness

Lao Hsiung", said Hsin Hsüeh to Fu Tze, "you have told us that our forgiveness of others should be so complete that it is as though the injury they did to us never existed. How are we to be sure that we have achieved this?"

Fu Tze arose and bowed low to Hsin Hsüeh, with an appearance of deep respect.

"My noble young friend", said the Sage, "please be aware of my gratitude to you for teaching me many things about the Way of Heaven."

Then Fu Tze left the garden.

"My question was a sincere one", said Hsin Hsüeh in great distress. "Why, then, should Fu Tze mock me and go away?"

"Fu Tze did not mock you", answered Yüan Chien. "A wise man knows that he learns from those he teaches, even as they learn from him.

"By expressing to you his humble recognition of this, Fu Tze told you that when you have exchanged places in your heart with your former enemy, so that you can hope sincerely that he will forgive you for your injustice to him, then you will know that your own forgiveness of him is complete."

The Mirror

"I do not understand how it is that the circumstances of our lives can change with the state of our inner being", said Hsin Hsüeh.

In reply, Fu Tze handed him a mirror.

Others

"I find that it is much easier to remember myself in the Way of Heaven when I am alone", said Hsi Fang. "When I am with others, I fall easily into the habits of thinking and acting that are characteristic of the Way of the World."

"Your problem", said Fu Tze, "is that you have been taught to consider others as people."

Arsenic

"I find my experiences and discussions in seeking wisdom and immortality so interesting that I wish to share them with my friends in conversation", said Ti Lang. "The few times I have done so, they have sometimes made very intelligent comments. Yet you say we should keep silent about these things. Why is this?"

"If you thrive on arsenic and yet it remains a poison to your friends, you do them no favour to share your arsenic with them", answered Fu Tze. "Also, you deplete your own supply of arsenic, on which you depend for your nourishment."

Appreciation of Beauty

Li Sun* demonstrates a devout sense of the spiritual nature of all things, yet she constantly exhibits scorn for your wisdom, and you do not appear to respect Li Sun", said Hsin Hsüeh. "How is it that two people so concerned with the nature of Heaven and Earth are thus antagonistic to each other?"

"When one fishes, it is not sufficient to skim the surface of the pool with the net", answered Fu Tze with a smile. "Li Sun's spirituality is like the exquisite sense of beauty of a man named Ya Ai.** Ya Ai so loved the beauty of nature that he camped one night in a public shelter within view of a majestic mountain, in order to admire its loveliness. The next morning it was necessary that Ya Ai move on, but he spent his final hour at that place sitting before the shelter and marveling at the beauty of the mountain, so that he might carry it with him in his memory.

"And because Ya Ai spent his last hour at that shelter marvelling at the beauty of the mountain, he left behind him the debris and garbage of his night's habitation to be cleaned away by the traveller who followed him."

* 麗猻
: "Elegant Monkey".

** 亞矮
: "Ugly Dwarf".

11. YA AI GAZES AT THE BEAUTIFUL MOUNTAIN

Love

"I have heard other teachers say that we must love all men as our brothers, yet you do not emphasize this", said I Chü. "Why is this?"

"When we swim in the garden, why does Hsin Hsüeh linger in the shallows of the pool?" asked Fu Tze with a smile.

"Because Hsin Hsüeh cannot swim yet", answered I Chü.

"Until you have learned to swim, you cannot save others from drowning, but must drown yourself if you attempt it", said Fu Tze.

When I Chü asked Yüan Chien about this reply, Yüan Chien said, "What Fu Tze meant was that you are not yet able to love in this way. When one is still in the Way of the World, he is able to love only those who are similar to him, for that is a reflection of his self-love.

"Therefore, it is first necessary to detach yourself from those you love and those you do not love, alike, lest you become infected by the fever of the soul that afflicts those who love the world. When from the bastion of yourself you can observe that fever in them and yet be able to say of them the words contained in the great 'I Ching',* 'no blame', then you will begin to be able to love them."

* 易經 : The classical ''Book of Changes''.

The Actress of Erhchiang

"I believe that Shen Chiao's misfortunes result from karma and that if she cannot resolve this karma in this life she must do so in a later reincarnation", said Ch'i P'eng. "But I Chü attributes her misfortunes to chance and contends that there will be no reincarnation into another life. Which is right?"

"Both and neither", said Fu Tze. "For which of you is qualified to prophesy the career of an actress in Erhchiang?"*

Ch'i P'eng and I Chü sought explanation of these words from Yüan Chien, and he answered:

"What is karma? The Sage has compared it to the manner in which an actress performs upon the stage: and who can say whether her ability springs from inner aptitude, from the chances of her life's experience, or from her own effort?

"When you speak of reincarnation, Fu Tze reminds you that there are three possibilities for an actress on the stage in Erhchiang. If she is competent, she will be retained in her role for as long as the public will support that play's performance there. If she is incompetent, she will be discharged and cannot find employment as an actress. If she strives and excels in her task, so that she becomes recognized as exceptional, her reputation will spread widely and she will be asked to play a larger and more rewarding role in a theatre in Peiching."

* A town of 5,000 population in Sinchiang Province.

Karma

"What is karma?" asked Hsin Hsüeh.

Fu Tze picked up a stone and tossed it into the air, so that when it fell, it struck him on the head and injured him slightly.

"That is karma", he said. "But it is also karma that I chose a small stone and not a boulder, which would have killed me. And it is also karma that I chose to answer your question by a demonstration, rather than in words."

"Karma, then would appear to be completely a consequence of our own choice", said Hsin Hsüeh.

"Not at all", replied the Sage. "For, had we been on the moon, I might have used a boulder for my demonstration, with impunity; and it is not by my choice that we are on earth, instead. Also, if I were not Fu Tze, I might have chosen to answer your question in words, and thereby have escaped this bruise on my head; but it was not by my choice that I was born Fu Tze."

"Since one is inevitably who and what he is, then, I cannot see how it is possible to change one's karma", said I Chü. "Will you tell us how this can be done?"

"Through injustice", answered Fu Tze.

"Therefore, if someone has injured you and you demand justice from him, you thereby establish a rule that you are subject to the same justice for an injury you do to someone else. But if you forgive that man, decreeing that he did not injure you and therefore owes you nothing, you have made him a different person in your eyes from the person that he was to you before, and thereby have changed yourself to a different person through your relationship to him.

"To act thus is not only to accept injustice to yourself, but may constitute grievous injustice to the one who has injured you; because, escaping just retribution for the injury he has done to you, he may be encouraged to commit further injury to someone else: and thus you have done injustice to yet this third person. But unquestionably, by becoming a different person yourself, you have changed your own karma."

I Chü, being offended by this reply asked Yüan Chien afterward how Fu Tze could have such a statement: "for", said I Chü, "is it not true that injustice brings its own punishment, even though one may escape the laws of men? And is not that itself karma?"

"That is true, but it is neither your question nor the answer to it", said Yüan Chien. "But it is in what you have said that there lies the meaning of Fu Tze's words. For what we are is measured by the way we see ourselves in relation to other men, and we do not see other people as they are, but only in relation to ourselves.

The Gordian Knot

Ti Lang and I Chü were discussing that story that Alexander the Great, confronted with the Gordian Knot and told that he who loosened it should conquer the world, found himself unable to untie it and therefore solved the problem by cutting it with his sword. I Chü insisted that the incident was historically true, while Ti Lang contended that it was simply a legend demonstrating Alexander's cleverness and determination to let nothing stand in the way of attaining his goal. They took their dispute before Fu Tze.

"Your argument is over a point of no importance", said Fu Tze. "If the incident actually occurred, it was not by necessity but by chance that it did so. Nor does it matter to you to know whether it occurred, Because a legend is as much a real fact as is a historical occurrence. Neither is of consequence except through the meaning it may convey."

"Then does not that support my viewpoint?" asked Ti Lang. "For I said it was a legend demonstrating Alexander's cleverness and determination."

"And of what consequence is it to us to know whether Alexander was clever and determined?" asked Fu Tze. "But you may also consider that Alexander's action in cutting the Gordian Knot demonstrated the mental qualities of a man with the imagination necessary to conquer the world by utilizing unorthodox methods.

"Yet his conquest was brief, because his unorthodox methods prevented the consolidation of the lands he had won into a stable social system before his death. Had he possessed the patience and understanding to untie the knot instead of cutting it, those qualities would have led him to consolidate his conquests and probably would also have bestowed upon him a life long enough to administer them.

"The story of the Gordian Knot is an image of Alexander's fate. And in this meaning, the story is of consequence to us, because it deals with mental qualities pertinent to the search for wisdom and immortality."

Authority

"How fortunate you are to have the company of a Sage!" exclaimed Hsia Yen,* a visitor to the garden. "Living far away in Shensi Province, I am distant from any Sage who could help me understand the Way of Heaven."

"It is remarkable that you have achieved the understanding that you have, then, without companionship in the Way of Heaven", said Yüan Chien.

"I am not without companionship in this search", said Hsia Yen. "My friend Yin Ming** is my companion, but he is not a Sage, only a poor artist. When we discuss questions of wisdom and immortality, both of us usually make equal contribution to the answers we reach."

"If Yin Ming attempted to give you authoritative answers about such questions, would you accept them?" asked Yüan Chien.

"No", answered Hsia Yen, "for I have seen too many pretenders to knowledge, therefore I would accept such authority only from a true Sage, such as Fu Tze."

"Yet", said Yüan Chien, "you believe Fu Tze to be a Sage only because there are 't'ao li' around him who respect his authority. Perhaps if Fu Tze discussed questions of wisdom and immortality with you in Shensi Province he could not speak to you authoritatively lest you consider him a pretender to knowledge, and he could help you only by joining you in making equal contributions to your own in your discussions."

* 瞎眼
: "Blind Man".

** 隱名
: "Hidden Name".

Vision

"Many who appear to be Sages are not, while a true Sage sometimes remains invisible in the guise of an ordinary man", said Hsin Hsüeh. "How, then, are we, who understand imperfectly, to determine who is truly a Sage?"

"The only way that you can see a Sage is with your 'I'," * replied Yüan Chien.

But Hsin Hsüeh still understood imperfectly, because he thought that Yüan Chien's answer was, "the only way you can see a Sage is with your eye." * *

* 自 : "Tzu", the self or essential nature.

** 眥 : "Tzu", the corner of the eye.

What Was Meant

"By the concept of God, I can only understand the totality of the Heaven and the Earth", said Ti Lang, "because that Existence which is absolute cannot exclude any part of existence as being not of itself."

"That is a good understanding", said Fu Tze.

"In that case", said Ti Lang, "what was meant by the Sage Chi Tu* when he said 'God is love'?"

"It is a definition", replied Fu Tze.

* 基督 : Jesus.

The Small Wisdom

"Before I began the search for wisdom and immortality, I felt that it was the most important thing possible in the world for me to do", said Hsin Hsüeh. "Now that I have embarked upon it, I am not tempted to abandon my search, yet I am unable to give any reason for seeking wisdom and immortality."

"That is because you have attained to a small wisdom", answered Fu Tze. "When you have attained to a larger wisdom, you will understand that a tree can have no goal except to grow."

The Quiet Place

"How can the wisdom and immortality that we seek be defined?" asked Hsin Hsüeh.

"It cannot be defined by any single definition", replied Fu Tze.

"But can you not give us one single definition of the many that must be applied to it", persisted Hsin Hsüeh.

"Very well", said the Sage. "In each of you there is a quiet place. Few find it. When you are in your quiet place, you cannot be disturbed or harmed, because nothing outside of you can penetrate it."

"But is this not death, rather than immortality?" asked I Chü. "For is not death the ultimate silence?"

"No", answered Fu Tze. "For noise is that which, having no

meaning itself, drowns out that which has meaning. And life is meaning.

"Therefore, death is noise, as disease is noise and hatred is noise and sorrow is noise. In the quiet place within you, all sounds are music, because noise cannot enter there."

Brothers

Once Fu Tze was travelling through Tsinghai Province, and came to a field where two brothers named Tzu,* one of them called Shih Hsin** and the other Hsü Hua, + were working together. At their invitation, Fu Tze lingered to share their midday meal of rice and eggs. During their conversation, Shih Hsin said:

"Though Hotien is far from here, I have heard of you, and it is said that you are a Sage. I myself have sought wisdom and immortality for many years, therefore I beg you to tell me some means whereby I may find them at last."

"Open your eyes and look around you", answered Fu Tze.

Shih Hsin did so, and exclaimed in amazement: "How beautiful! Wisdom and immortality are here and now, and I see that I have lived in the midst of them for a long time. Why could I not see this before?"

* 自
: "Oneself" or "the self".

** 實心
: "True Heart" or "Honest".

\+ 虛華
: "Vain".

"Only because, in your search for wisdom and immortality, you habituated yourself to a search for something you had not yet acquired", said Fu Tze. "After searching for so long, you did not know how to break the habit of searching."

Shih Hsin thereupon turned to his brother and said to him: "The wisdom and immortality we have sought for so long are here around us, my brother. Just open you eyes and see how beautiful they are!"

But when Hsü Hua opened his eyes and looked around him, he screamed in terror and shut them quickly again.

"How can you call this wisdom and immortality?" he cried. "It is the most horrible sight I have ever beheld, and certainly must be the Hell to which damned souls are consigned!"

Puzzled, Shi Hsin turned to Fu Tze and asked, "How is this! for surely my brother and I are both here in the same place, and yet when I follow your admonition and open my eyes, I see only beauty."

"Ah", replied the Sage, "but I said that to you, not to your brother."

The Temptation

"Surely even Sages face temptation in the Way of Heaven", Yüan Chien said once to Fu Tze. "Would you be willing to tell me, First Born, what is your own greatest stumbling block?"

"Indeed", answered Fu Tze. "It is the temptation to believe that I am a Sage."

The Welfare of the Community

"Since the Way of Heaven is truer and simpler than the Way of the World, once it is comprehended, why has it not become the normal manner of life for mankind?" asked Hsin Hsüeh.

"Because of the welfare of the community", answered Fu Tze.

"I do not understand how this can be so", said Hsin Hsüeh.

"Once, according to a story that I have heard, men and women were truly human", said Fu Tze. "Being human, they were present in themselves and, because they were different individuals, they differed in their characteristics and in their attitudes. Since they differed in their characteristics and in their attitudes, they also differed in the state of their welfare, for such is the Way of Heaven.

"Among these differing individuals there were those whose difference from their fellows was that they wished to know with certainty what circumstances the morrow would bring, so that they might plan their courses of action accordingly. But such certainty was not possible to them, because of the differing nature of individuals. For example, a man who wished to buy a pig could not know how much money to take with him, for one man might give him a pig without recompense, while another might demand more money for a pig than he carried. To those who wished to know what circumstances the morrow would bring, such uncertainty in the price of pigs seemed an intolerable reflection of the difference in the state of welfare among different individuals.

"Therefore, those who wished to know with certainty what circumstances the morrow would bring consulted a powerful magician to see if some solution could not be found to this intolerable situation of differences among individuals.

"The magician responded that he possessed a formula whereby men and women could be transformed from human individuals into machines, resembling men and women in every respect except that programs of predictable action could be patterned into them, suppressing their individual autonomy to an extent adequate to cause them to respond alike to the same stimuli in most instances. The magician's formula involved extracting each person's soul and exiling it to a realm of fantasy, where it would be unable to influence the mind and body left behind in the world of reality but would imagine that it was fulfilling its own unique destiny.

"The manner in which each individual person's soul was persuaded to absent itself from his mind and body was through utilization of two natural human tendencies, both of which originated, not in man's humanity, but in the social nature of his animal ancestors. The first of these tendencies was the tendency to attempt to persuade others of one's superior importance and ability, so that those others would be inclined to coöperate in fulfilling one's personal desires for fear of giving offense to a worthy and powerful person. The second of these tendencies was the tendency to imitate others whom one believed to possess superior importance and ability, in order that one might, by doing as they did, become as important and able as they.

"Those who desired predictability in the conduct of others agreed to the terms of the magician, for their own purposes; and thereby they also became machines, through the necessity of adapting themselves to the programs of action they designed for others, in order to make use of those programs. In this way, all humanity was gradually transformed from individual men and women into machines, and their souls banished into an imaginery world where nothing actually happened.

"Now you must understand, Hsin Hüeh, that this is only a story that I have heard told, and thus is not necessarily true. But it is true that men and women exist as individual human beings only in the Way of Heaven. In the Way of the World, because of the actions of that powerful magician, they are only machines programmed to courses of predictable action, while they themselves are absent, asleep and dreaming about things that do not really happen."

Some other books from Coombe Springs Press

THE SHERBORNE THEME TALKS SERIES

Working with Themes.

Themes are more than ideas to be thought about. They are aspects of practical wisdom: how to live. This wisdom can be awakened by making an active contact with our own experience. Observation is not enough and thinking is totally inadequate. The aim we have is to work towards a new practical understanding of life so that we can begin to live differently. The relation of our inner life to the external world, our bodies, other people and Nature needs to change. The new life cannot be reduced to a set of rules or commandments which can only dictate behaviour. It has to be discovered in action, in the hazards of life; and usually through many small moments when something is revealed to us that we cannot doubt.

John G. Bennett was a master at conducting theme meetings and could draw out the most profound lessons from the most faltering of contributions. He helped people to see for themselves the practical core of the spiritual path and avoid the twin evils of doubt and philosophising.

The Sherborne Theme Talks Series are taken from tape recordings of meetings at Sherborne House between 1972 and 1975. We are able to publish only a small selection from the hundreds of tapes.

Number One – THE FIRST LIBERATION

Number Two – NOTICING

Number Three – MATERIAL OBJECTS

Number Four – FOOD

THE TRANSFORMATION OF MAN SERIES

The Monographs are largely based on lecture talks given by John G. Bennett between October 1921 and December 1974.

Many of the themes and ideas developed in these talks were the foundation for an important series of books which he began writing shortly before his death in December 1974. The aim was to show a new view of the world, an utterly positive one, based on the firm conviction that man must transform himself and that this transformation is to some degree possible for every man and woman. Many of the ideas are taken from Gurdjieff, but have been developed further and sometimes superseded.

Number One	– GURDJIEFF TODAY
Number Two	– THE ENNEAGRAM
Number Three	– SEX
Number Four	– THE SEVENFOLD WORK
Number Five	– THE IMAGE OF GOD IN WORK
Number Six	– JOHN G. BENNETT'S TALKS ON BEELZEBUB'S TALES
Number Seven	– NEEDS OF A NEW AGE COMMUNITY